ANGER MANAGEMENT FOR TEENS

HOW TO OVERCOME ANGER AND TAKE CONTROL OF YOUR LIFE.

JENA ROGERS

Ask questions that help them find the solution.

Put the matter on the table.

Try to be credible.

Learn about your child's issue and/or diagnosis.

CHAPTER SEVEN.

CONCLUSION.

INTRODUCTION.

It can feel very difficult to be an adolescent. Adolescence may be a time of flux, of movement between childhood and adulthood, and of giant physical, emotional, and psychological changes. It's also a time of beginning to understand and accept you, and also to know and grapple with the important moral issues and dilemmas of the planet, and this will be disturbing and challenging.

Some teenagers seem to get through all this, but others find themselves in remarkable difficulty. Half all lifetime psychological state disorders start by the mid-teens, including psychotic disorders, depression, mental disorder and substance misuse and its consequences. People handle frustration and stress in several ways due to specific situations, outside issues and personalities. Some get depressed, some become more resilient and a few get angry. Anger can cause anguish and family dysfunction, and may lead onto other more significant issues.

Many teenagers feel angry, and develop complications managing their anger.

In this book we discuss the actual problems of anger management in teenagers, and proffer solutions.

?

CHAPTER ONE.

ANGER.

Anger may be a normal human emotion, a process of releasing mental and emotional pressure. It is often seen as a defense reaction, a coping mechanism, a way of displacing other difficult emotions, an inexpensive response in some circumstances.

Getting angry is normal, but letting anger get the simplest of you isn't. Anger isn't present alone. It's often triggered by other difficult feelings like hurt, frustration or sadness, and may be a way of deflecting or avoiding these emotions. Sometimes going to the basis explanation for the anger can defuse it, by analyzing the important problem and learning to treat it rationally.

Anger is often overwhelming, and it is often difficult to understand what to try to do with it. Although anger can produce physical and emotional discomfort, it's the way of expressing it which will cause the issues. Anger results in acting instead of thinking, and therein lies the problem.

A teenager who can't deal with angry feelings may feel a robust desire to act directly on the emotions, even when it puts them or others in danger or leads them to actions which, when not angry they might consider disreputable.

Dealing with the results is then much of a dilemma than the anger itself.

Anger produces or moves outward, usually towards another person. It tends to let out onto people or objects. This will involve punching inanimate objects, stepping into fights and upending much-needed friendships. People can make poor decisions once they are angry. Managing anger involves helping the teenager understand that anger may be a normal feeling, but the way they prefer to handle it is a choice. They require help to seek out different strategies that won't cause harm or destroy their life.

Anger is a component of our emotional spectrum, and may be a normal, healthy emotional response to outside stressors. In fact, anger helps us to "deal" with threats once we feel crossed or challenged. It's once we let our emotions effect our actions that anger can become harmful in teens. While anger may be a normal emotional response to outside stressors, teens got to learn healthy coping mechanisms now, before they reach adulthood. Teens got to know that it's not wrong or bad to feel angry, but that they can't let the anger consume them or control their actions. This is often vital to making sure that your child's anger remains a legitimate emotional reaction instead of escalating into violence, defiant behavior, or rage.

CHAPTER TWO.

SIGNS OF PROBLEMATIC ANGER.

Sometimes, as a parent, you're so on the brink of things that it's difficult to be objective about your child's anger issues. Some parents are quick to ignore anger as a traditional a part of the teenage experience, while others grow very concerned over emotional outbursts and acts of defiance. Remember that anger may be a normal, healthy response that's innate in attribute, and is really a part of the fight or flight response. Yelling, arguing, name-calling, and crying can all be normal teenage responses to anger—in as much as they are do not build up to violence or rage. However, if your child regularly experiences the "red flag" signs below, his or her anger issues may have to be addressed;

• stepping into physical confrontations at college or at home with siblings.

• Constant arguing with parents, teachers, peers, siblings, etc.

• Excessive emotional outbursts and fury.

• Persistent irritability.

• Irrationality.

• Bullying.

• Relationship/dating violence.

• Verbal threats.

• Being brutish to younger siblings or pets (those who can't defend themselves).

• Physical violence.

• Destroying property.

• Self-harm (cutting, burning, etc.) this is often a symbol of depression, which may be a culprit of teenage anger, emotional outbursts, and defiance.

If your teen's anger goes beyond the traditional, emotional response to outside stressors, and your child exhibits the signs above, a rational next step is to consult his or her physician or mental healthcare provider.

CHAPTER THREE.

<u>Ways to Assist Your Teen with Their Anger Problem.</u>

Some teens aren't emotionally equipped to handle anxiety, depression, conflict, or trauma in a healthy way. While many parents' first instinct is to "control" or "manage" their teen's anger, it's important to recollect that you simply cannot control someone else's emotions or actions. What you'll do, is put in place realistic expectations and consequences, and provide your child the tools to more effectively deal with his or her negative emotions.

□□□□ □□□□ □□□□ □□□□ □ □□□□□□□ □□□□□□□ □□ □□□□□□□ □□□□□.

Helping your teen to seek out an outlet for anger may be a good way to supply a healthier coping mechanism for negative emotions. Most are different, so see what appeals to your child. Healthy outlets for anger can include:

• Sports

• Exercise

• Yoga

• Writing a journal

• playing loud, angry music.

□□□□□□□□
□□□□□□□□□□□,
□□□□□, □□□
□□□□□□□□□□□.

If you haven't already, initiate clear rules and consequences for breaking said rules. It's important to converse once you and your teen are both calm, cool, and picked up. This may make sure that you've got a rational, non-judgmental conversation together with your son or daughter. Explain that anger may be a valid emotional reaction that everybody experiences which you're more concerned about the negative, angry behaviors that they're displaying-- not the emotion itself.

□□□□ □□□ □□ □□□ □□□□□ □□ □□□ □□□□□□□.

When your child has calmed down, ask them and check out to seek out what's really bothering them. Trying to have a reasonable conversation while your child is having an emotional outburst or fit of rage is going to be counter-productive, and should cause you to become frustrated also. Ask if something wrong at school or with classmates. Hear his or her problems without judgment; just remember, they'll become angry, or they'll not tell you. It's still important to point out that you simply do care.

☐☐☐☐☐☐ ☐☐☐☐☐☐ ☐☐☐☐·

Spending an excessive amount of time on electronic devices (smart phones, computer game consoles, tablets, etc.) can hinder your child's sleep hygiene. Poor sleeping patterns can cause irritability, and further vulnerability to angry outbursts. Additionally, it's important to watch your teens' device habits, as exposure to violent TV shows, video games, and films can increase the likelihood of violent behavior and outbursts also.

☐☐☐☐ ☐☐ ☐☐☐☐☐☐☐·

Make sure that you simply are using healthy coping mechanisms to checkmate your anger. Children learn what they live. Additionally, if your teen sees you become aggressive once you are angry, your teen might imagine that this is often an appropriate emotional response. This is often especially important to recollect when your teen has an outburst. As difficult as it sounds, remaining calm during your child's outbursts will help diffuse things. You'll teach more about anger management skills together with your behavior than your words.

□□□□□

□□□□□□□□□□□.

Anger can come from the shortage of being assertive enough. Help teenagers to stand up for themselves - to ask without demanding.

□□□□□ □□□□□□

□□□□□□.

Teens got to know appropriate ways to handle angry feelings. Help them find ways to settle down e.g. going for a walk, singing of songs. Help them with problem solving. If someone understands there are several possible solutions to a complication, they're more likely to spend a couple of minutes thinking it through. Identifying the pros and cons of solutions is a crucial problem anger management skill.

CHAPTER FOUR.
The Importance of Early Intervention.

Although some parents are only too quick to write off teen anger as their child being a "moody teen" or "hormonal," parents should seek outside intervention if their child exhibits behavior indicating that his or her anger is out of control. Those signs could signify an underlying problem, such an undiagnosed psychological state issue or an unresolved conflict or trauma that must be addressed. If left unsettled, anger can escalate and cause many problems during a young person's life, including:

• Problems at school.

• Trouble with the authorities.

• Becoming absorbed with anger; holding grudges and not having the ability to drop issues in the past when others have wronged them.

• Damaging themselves or others.

• Isolation.

• Strained family and peer relationships.

In addition to those immediate risks, teens who don't receive help for his or her unresolved anger issues are in danger for developing lifelong maladaptive patterns/unhealthy coping mechanisms for anger which will be harder to vary later in life. These could lead on to more serious problems down the road, like violence.

In addition to helping your teen learning healthier coping mechanisms for his or her anger, early intervention is additionally vital in helping your teen resolve whatever fundamental issues are behind his or her anger problem. For instance, if your teen is exhibiting anger and emotional outbursts thanks to an undiagnosed mental disorder, it's far better to deal with this issue in adolescence, instead of waiting until he or she has reached adulthood. Not only does your child have the potential to develop unhealthy coping mechanisms for anger, but he or she could develop unhealthy coping mechanisms to handle anxiety also.

When an adolescent wants to speak about anger issues then, as in any consultation, you would like to specialize in the matter, determine what's been happening and assist in finding solutions. Building rapport is extremely important, but watch out for promising absolute confidentiality – you'll hear something that you simply cannot keep confidential.

□□□□□□ □□ □□□□.

Use active listening. Allow them to talk.

Understand their life situation.

Make time: make it clear you've got time.

Acknowledge their feelings. Put the matter on the table and appearance at it together.

Discover what they feel and actions taken when they're angry.

Ask what negative outcomes have there been.

Find out what the youth feels about their family. It helps gain confidence and makes an idea.

Find out who they speak to (ask about online influences).

□□□□□ □□□□□□□□□□.

Be aware of worrying features, such as:

Self-harm, interest in suicide, brutality to animals, disordered thoughts and concepts, suggestions of internet grooming, isolation from peers and family, abuse of drugs, alcohol, risky sexual behavior.

□□□□ □□ □□□□.

Tell them that anger is a modified physical condition.

Discuss how this feels. Describe how anger is an emotion not an act.

Discuss the difference between anger and aggression. Attempt to have mutual understanding around the incontrovertible fact that some actions are harmful and would have to be avoided.

Make it clear that you simply would really like to assist.

CHAPTER FIVE.

<u>Effective Treatment Options.</u>

Some parents will hesitate to look for treatment, ignoring problematic anger as "teenage dread" or "growing pains." If your son or daughter's anger and emotional outbursts became problematic, then early intervention is vital to helping him or her handle anger in a healthy way.

☐☐☐☐☐ ☐☐☐☐☐☐☐☐☐ ☐☐☐☐☐☐☐.

Apart from regular psychotherapy sessions, your child's healthcare provider may suggest anger management classes also. These classes cover effective, healthy coping mechanisms to assist your teen recognize angry feelings and contain his or her anger in-the-moment. Your child may learn breathing techniques, relaxation skills, and proper ways to precise angry feelings to others.

CHAPTER SIX.

THE ROLE OF PARENTS.

Teenagers often don't want to speak to their parents. This lack of conversation leaves many parents feeling excluded from their adolescent's world. There are some strategies parents can use to encourage teenagers to talk:

□□□□□□ □□□ □□□□□□□.

When your teenager converses with you, don't jump in and automatically share your opinion. Instead, reflect what you hear to point out that you're really listening.

□□□□ □□□□□□□ □□□ □□□□□□□□.

We are less patient with our families than with strangers. Avoid using harsh words that you simply wouldn't tell a stranger. Don't answer disrespect from your teen with equally disrespectful behavior. You're the adult.

☐☐☐☐☐☐☐☐☐☐ ☐☐☐ ☐☐☐☐ ☐☐☐☐·

This doesn't mean you've got to agree. For instance, 'I can see how frustrated you are.'

☐☐☐ ☐☐ ☐☐☐☐☐☐ ☐☐☐ ☐☐☐ ☐☐☐ ☐☐☐☐ ☐☐ ☐☐☐☐·

If your current attempts to speak to your teen don't seem to be working, break the pattern and check out something new, see if it encourages him or her to speak.

31

□□□□□□ □□□□ □□□□ □□□ □□□□.

Listening will get you much further than talking. Be willing to listen to what your teen has got to say. Use active listening skills to point out that you simply actually need to know. This suggests things like repeating words back, prompting them to continue, mirroring their posture and concentrating on them.

□□□ □□□□□□□□□ □□□□ □□□□ □□□□ □□□□ □□□ □□□□□□□□.

Open questions are better than closed questions, generally. Be curious and interested, not nosy or probing.

□□□ □□□ □□□□□□ □□ □□□ □□□□□.

Teens got to start learning the way to solve problems but you'll help. Don't give the matter straight back to them but don't keep it either. Put it on an imaginary table between you and run through it together.

□□□ □□ □□ □□□□□□□□.

One common barrier is that teens think their parents can't possibly relate to what they're experiencing. Saying 'I was a teenager just like you' won't help.

Instead of telling them that you simply understand, show them you're trying to know.

□□□□□ □□□□□ □□□□ □□□□□'□ □□□□□ □□□/□□ □□□□□□□□□.

Find out more about whatever has been troubling your child and/or contributing to his or her emotional outbursts and problematic anger. If your child has been diagnosed with depression or it seems that your child still hasn't come to terms with your divorce, determine more about the way to help. Doing this may assist you to form informed decisions during and after treatment. Research, read, attend support groups and parenting classes. During this age of extensive information, it shouldn't be hard to find out more about your child's struggles. Learning the maximum amount as you can from your child about what the struggle has been like for them can help them feel your support.

CHAPTER SEVEN.

CONCLUSION.

It is important to be aware of the possible presence of an unhappy teenager with an apparently trivial problem, and to be prepared to ask open questions.

If you're concerned about your son or daughter's problematic anger, emotional outbursts, and acts of defiance, it's important to acknowledge when anger goes too far. Early intervention is vital to giving your child the tools to successfully manage his or her emotions during a healthy way as an adult. There are situations when anger isn't normal or healthy. If you're angry more often than you're not angry, you'll be battling an anger problem. Also, if you're acting aggressively or violently, this is often a sign that you simply might need professional help to manage your anger better. There's no shame in reaching out for help; managing anger are some things that adults got to work on, too. It's better to urge a handle thereon now before you reach adulthood.

Anger has the potential to negatively affect your job and your adult relationships, therefore the skills that you simply learn now can have a lifetime impact. If you would like help controlling your anger, ask your parents or another trusted adult. Your physician also can refer you to a psychological health specialist who can assist you get to rock bottom of what's causing your anger and teach you strategies to regulate it so it doesn't result in it controlling you.

Manufactured by Amazon.ca
Bolton, ON